Skills and Strategies

Strategies

for **Learning**

11-14

Successful Learners

Confident Individuals

Effective Contributors

Responsible Citizens

D1368922

M-C McInally — Eric Summers

Text © 2007 M-C McInally and Eric Summers

Design and layout © 2007 Leckie & Leckie Ltd

Cover image © Caleb Rutherford

01/310507

ISBN 978-1-84372-478-0

Published by

Leckie & Leckie Ltd, 3rd Floor, 4 Queen Street, Edinburgh EH2 1JE

tel: 0131 220 6831   fax: 0131 225 9987

enquiries@leckieandleckie.co.uk   www.leckieandleckie.co.uk

Edited by

Tony Wayte, Fiona MacDonald

Special thanks to

Project One Publishing Solutions (content development and editorial),

The Partnership Publishing Solutions (design and layout), Eduardo Iturralde (Illustrations),

Andrew Burnet (proofreading), Caleb Rutherford (cover)

A CIP Catalogue record for this book is available from the British Library.

Leckie & Leckie is a division of Huveaux plc.

Contents

Introduction

This is a book about making the most of your life, both in and out of school. What you learn *in* the classroom can and should help you enjoy things elsewhere. The knowledge, skills and interests which you can bring *into* the classroom will enable you to get much more out of your various school subjects. What you learn in one classroom, you should be able to use in the next.

Everything is connected!

It's easy to look at your daily and weekly routines and see lots of separate bits of life – a maths class, a games lesson, a trip to the climbing wall with friends, tea with your auntie. But instead of keeping everything in separate boxes, you can make sure that experience gained in one activity is used to increase the pleasure you get from all the other things you do. If you are going to lead a full life, you must try to be:

✔ a successful learner because in order to understand a world that is changing at tremendous speed you will always have to be absorbing new ideas and information

✔ a confident individual because believing in yourself will make you healthier, happier and better able to make the most of your talents

✔ an effective contributor because you should use the talents you undoubtedly have to make your classrooms, teams and clubs as good as they can possibly be

✔ a responsible citizen because it is good to show respect for other people, to care for the environment and to be proud of the community in which you live.

Learning successfully increases confidence, makes your contributions more effective and makes you think about responsible citizenship. Being a good citizen makes you feel good about yourself, which encourages you to contribute to activities, which will make you a more successful learner. Everything is connected.

A full life is one in which you see and take advantage of the connections. This book will help you do just that.

Moving from primary to secondary school

If you are in Primary 7, you will be going up to secondary school after the summer holidays. Your new secondary school will make every effort to welcome you. You will get the chance to visit the school for one or more days while you are still in Primary 7 and most schools hold an evening to explain things to your parents. There will also be a booklet given to you, which will provide lots of information about *the big school*. You will have lots of new hopes and dreams for the future but you might also be a bit nervous and anxious about leaving a school where you feel safe and comfortable for one where there will be lots of new names and faces.

You might worry about the size of the secondary school. It might seem very big after primary school and you might worry about getting lost. First year classes are often given senior pupil guides for the first week or so and you will quite quickly get to know your way around. You will probably be given a map of the school as well. Make sure you keep this handy and don't be embarrassed to use it. You'll probably have a planner or daily binder you can keep the map in.

Children like to tease one another, so you might hear of some 'horror stories' about what goes on at secondary school. Most of the stories you hear will be nonsense, but if you do find yourself having problems, like being picked on or not being able to cope with the work, you must do something about it. Tell someone you're not happy. You can read more about what to do on pages 33 to 35 of this book. Your new teachers will be keeping a look out for you and will certainly want to know if any older pupils are behaving badly. Most schools will pair you up with a *buddy*, who will probably be a sixth year or a senior pupil who will meet you regularly to check you are settling in, make sure you can find everything and help you get to know the canteen, sports facilities and clubs at lunchtimes. Buddies are good to talk to and often help you with your first lot of homework.

Getting to know new people is exciting. But if you are usually quiet and shy it might be a bit scary being in a class with boys and girls from other primary schools. Just remember that you will not be alone. Secondary schools try hard to make sure that pupils have at least two boys or girls from the same primary school in each secondary class. Remember also that the other people in the class will be feeling a bit strange as well. You will all get to know each other quickly enough.

Be positive. Think of the new friends you are going to make, the new subjects you are going to study and the extra-curricular activities to get involved in. For a few days you might wish you were back in primary – by the October break you will certainly not!

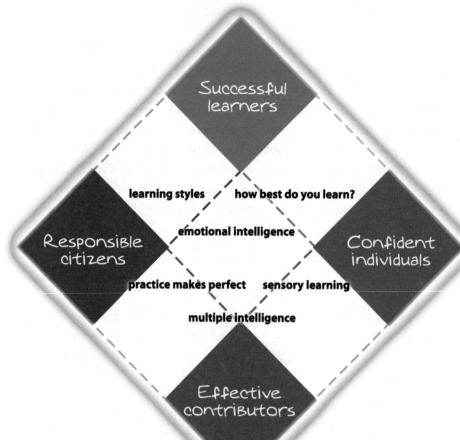

The amazing brain

Believe it or not, you can train your brain to work better. In this chapter you'll read about:

- ✔ **learning styles** and you'll be able to work out which style is best for you
- ✔ **the structure of the brain** and why it is important
- ✔ **multi-sensory learning** which can help you remember more!
- ✔ **multiple intelligences** which can explain why different people have different talents and abilities
- ✔ **emotional intelligence** and how it can help you cope with difficulties and lead a happier life.

Knowing about all this will help you become a more successful learner and a more confident individual. When things need to be done, you will be able to make **effective contributions**. Understanding yourself will help you **act responsibly**.

How do you learn best?

To find out how you learn best, you must ask
yourself this question:

> **When do I
> learn best?**

Do you learn best in a uncomfortable and unfriendly room, or in an
environment that is comfortable and friendly, which helps you to think and join
in? Think about your classroom or your bedroom. Is it bright and airy and full
of pictures and colour?

Your brain works best when you are at the right temperature to keep you
comfortable without being too hot or too cold. It will be ready for work when
you've eaten properly and taken the right amount of exercise. Brains like to be
used, so you need to do different activities using all your senses of touch, sight,
hearing, taste and smell to help you to learn.

This chapter will help you understand how you learn, so you can put together
your own **learning profile** to help make your brain become even more
amazing!

We all have individual **learning styles** and **intelligences**. You might know
someone who seems to be good at everything. You might know someone who
is *great* at science or maths but not so good at English and maybe *very bad*
at sport. You may feel you are better at one thing than another or you may
already be saying 'I *can't* do that!' Let's explain.

Learning styles

We all have our own learning profile, made up of:

✔ our learning style – the way we learn
✔ our multiple intelligences
✔ the ways we interact with our environment.

Understanding **how you learn** will help you increase your ability to **learn more effectively** and to become a **smarter learner**.

How the brain works

The brain has a **left side** and a **right side**. Each side works slightly differently to help us work things out. Most of us use one side more than the other, although a few people do use both sides equally.

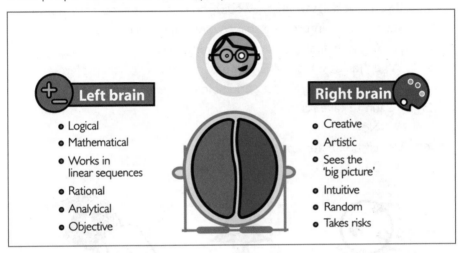

Left brain
- Logical
- Mathematical
- Works in linear sequences
- Rational
- Analytical
- Objective

Right brain
- Creative
- Artistic
- Sees the 'big picture'
- Intuitive
- Random
- Takes risks

Each side of the brain does different things and this shows in the way you behave. Have a look at the table and see which side of the brain you think you use most.

Left side (verbal)	Right side (visual)
✔ speaks using few gestures	✔ speaks using gestures
✔ responds to word meanings	✔ responds to tone of voice
✔ likes sequences and order	✔ prefers randomness and no order
✔ responds to logic	✔ responds to emotion
✔ plans ahead	✔ impulsive
✔ recalls people's names	✔ recalls people's faces
✔ prefers to be on time	✔ ignores time and sits with back to clock
✔ prefers quiet study	✔ prefers music when studying
✔ prefers bright light	✔ prefers to move around

The amazing brain

Brain quiz

Let's see which is your dominant side by doing a quick brain test.

Read the following statements and questions. Circle the answer which better describes you.

1   If you have a jigsaw puzzle would you sort out the corners first or start with an interesting shape/colour and work around it?
    A   Corners first   B   Interesting shape/colour

2   When taking a test, which type of questions do you prefer?
    A   Written   B   Multiple choice/True/False

3   It's fun to take risks.
    A   No   B   Yes

4   Which box matches box 1?
    A   Box 2   B   Box 3

5   Do you have a place for everything and keep everything in its place?
    A   Yes   B   No

6   My thinking is like pictures going through my head.
    A   No   B   Yes

7   Is it easier for you to remember people's faces or people's names?
    A   People's names   B   People's faces

8   When you are speaking, do you use hand gestures?
    A   No   B   Yes

9   Do you use your imagination when you work?
    A   No   B   Yes

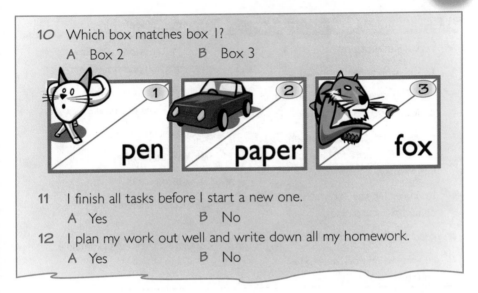

10 Which box matches box 1?
    A Box 2   B Box 3

11 I finish all tasks before I start a new one.
    A Yes   B No
12 I plan my work out well and write down all my homework.
    A Yes   B No

To find your score, give yourself I point each time you answered **B**. Add up the Bs and see where you are on the scale below.

Left-brained ⟵ ⟶ **Right-brained**

| I | 2 | 3 | 4 | 5 | 6 | 7 | 8 | 9 | 10 | II | 12 |

The higher the score the more right-brained you are. The lower the score the more left-brained you are. If you score in the middle, you are a balanced left- and right-brained learner.

www.leckieandleckie.co.uk
This quiz can be downloaded from ACE Study Skills pages of the
Leckie & Leckie Learning Lab website.

A **left-brained learner** prefers to learn by *chunking* (using small pieces of information at a time). They like structure to their learning and clear instructions.

A **right-brained learner** prefers to learn by getting the *big* picture of the topic before going into the detail.

The amazing brain

Left-brained learners prefer:	Right-brained learners prefer:
✔ verbal instructions	✔ visual instructions (like PowerPoint presentation and flow charts)
✔ talking when problem-solving	
✔ checking to see they are doing the task properly	✔ 'seeing' or being told what the overall picture is going to be like
✔ receiving written information, so they can re-read instructions and information	✔ making their own choice of tasks
	✔ using creativity
	✔ suggesting ideas
✔ having order and structure – they cannot work in a mess	✔ using colour, pictures, graphs and music
✔ keeping their jotters and notes tidy	✔ working to their own timetable
✔ knowing when work has to be handed in	

If you're like most people, you probably use one side of your brain more than the other. It may help you to try and use your less dominant side sometimes to improve your performance with some tasks.

Multi-sensory learning

Now you are a bit more familiar with the way the brain works , it is time to introduce to you the idea of multi-sensory learning. We talked earlier about using all your senses when you are learning. There are three senses which are most useful, and you'll probably be either a **visual learner**, an **auditory learner**, or a **kinaesthetic learner**.

> Visual learners **like to see pictures and images.**
>
> Auditory learners **like to hear stories being read aloud, music, and songs.**
>
> Kinaesthetic learners **like to do things through movement, touch and feelings.**

When a **visual** learner asks a question they will say:

> *Do you see? or Is that clear?*

When an **auditory** learner asks a question they will say:

> *Does that sound right? or Are you listening?*

When a **kinaesthetic** learner asks a question they will say:

> *Does that feel right? or Have you got a handle on that?*

If you know about the way you use your senses, you can use them to become a smarter learner.

Visual learners prefer:	Auditory learners prefer:	Kinaesthetic learners prefer:
Written instructions	Spoken instructions	Hands-on activities such as practical work
Images and pictures	Radio and soundtracks	Art and crafts
Posters	Group work with discussions	Drama
DVDs and movies	Debates	Sport
		Writing

Multiple intelligences

We all show our intelligence in different ways, and knowing about the differences can help you understand what you're naturally good at and what you need to think about a bit more carefully. It is thought there are at least seven different ways to show our intelligence. The different intelligences are:

- ✔ Linguistic – word clever
- ✔ Mathematical – number clever
- ✔ Visual – picture clever
- ✔ Musical – musically clever
- ✔ Kinaesthetic – body movement clever
- ✔ Interpersonal – people clever
- ✔ Intrapersonal – self clever

Let's find out where your strengths are in the **multiple intelligences quiz**. Look at the statements in the quiz and think about whether you agree with the statements. Score 5 marks if you fully agree with the statement, and 1 if you fully disagree. Score 2, 3 or 4 if you're somewhere between.

1   Fully disagree
2   Partly disagree
3   Neither disagree or agree
4   Partly agree
5   Fully agree

	Statement	Score
1	I always do tasks one step at a time	
2	I can remember number plates on cars	
3	I have a good vocabulary and speak confidently	
4	I am good at writing stories	
5	I am good at sport	
6	I know the type of personality I have	
7	I am friendly and enjoy being in company	
8	I listen to others when they are talking and can repeat what they have said	
9	I like to be practical and work with crafts	
10	I work well when listening to music	
11	I love solving puzzles	
12	I speak to myself and talk through my thoughts	
13	I enjoy singing and dancing	
14	I learn better if I can see things as a movie rather than read a book	
15	I am a caring person and always try to be sensitive to others	
16	I am happy to work on my own	
17	I try to be organised and prioritise tasks	
18	I need to value what I am doing	

19	I often go for a walk or think things through when exercising	
20	I work well in a group	
21	I have a good sense of direction	
22	I am good at making friends see sense	
23	I can memorise music and play without sheets in front of me	
24	I enjoy taking objects apart and putting them back together	
25	I enjoy board games	
26	I like peace and quiet when I am working	
27	I can identify different kinds of musical instruments	
28	I like patterns and rhythms	
29	I enjoy being a team member	
30	I am good at remembering details	
31	I am a fidget	
32	I work well when I have to work out the problem myself	
33	I enjoy making music	
34	I love maths	
35	I am confident and make my own mind up	

Now add up your scores. Different questions tell you different things about your multiple intelligences.

Intelligence	Questions	Score
Linguistic (word clever)	3, 4, 8, 12, 20	
Mathematical (number clever)	1, 11, 17, 28, 34	
Visual/image (picture clever)	2, 14, 21, 24, 30	
Musical (musically clever)	10, 13, 23, 27, 33	
Kinaesthetic (body movement clever)	5, 9, 16, 19, 31	
Interpersonal (people clever)	7, 15, 22, 25, 29	
Intrapersonal (self clever)	6, 18, 26, 32, 35	

The amazing brain

To find out your multiple intelligence profile

Colour in each segment of the spider's web with your total score for that area. This gives you a picture of your multiple intelligences.

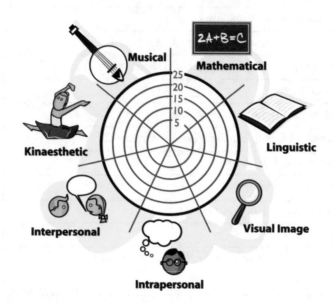

www.leckieandleckie.co.uk

This quiz can be downloaded from ACE Study Skills pages of the Leckie & Leckie Learning Lab website.

Practice does make perfect

Don't worry if your score is low in some parts of the spider's web. All this shows is where your natural strengths and weaknesses are. The good news is there are some simple ways to try to improve some of your weaknesses. Use the list to see what you can do to improve your score in any particular intelligence.

Linguistic intelligence

✔ **Learn to use a dictionary.** Every time you come across a new word, look it up in a dictionary and learn more about it - what does it mean, and where does it come from? Put it into a sentence and try it out on someone.

✔ **Read out loud.** Use your spare time to read to a younger brother or sister or read a piece of the newspaper to an adult. If that is not possible, just read aloud to yourself and get used to your own reading voice.

✔ **Read a section from a book,** then try to explain to someone what it was all about.

Mathematical intelligence

✔ **Look for patterns.** There are patterns everywhere - in words, wallpaper, floor coverings, curtains etc.

✔ **Keep your room tidy.** Sort and organise your stuff into categories or boxes so they are easy to find. See Chapter 3 for help with this.

✔ **Use mindmaps.** You'll read more about this in Chapter 3.

Visual intelligence

✔ **Colour code your notes** to help you read them more easily.

✔ **Draw a mindmap of a chapter in a book you have just read,** then describe your drawing to someone

✔ **Try crosswords and word puzzles.** They will help you make connections between words.

✔ **Practise spelling with someone.** Say a word, then spell it, then write it down.

✔ **Read books with plenty of colour and pictures.** This will help you stay with the text and finish the book.

Musical intelligence

✔ **Use a favourite song to help you remember something for a test.** It will feel like a leisure activity rather than a chore.

✔ **Sing and clap out the rhythm to a song.** This will help you coordinate your actions.

✔ **Use music when you are working.** This will help you concentrate on your work as you will be relaxed.

✔ **Practise saying difficult words.** This will help your confidence and work the muscles in your mouth.

Kinaesthetic intelligence

✔ Change where you write. Use different areas for different subjects to keep you mobile and active. Do your Maths in the living room, your English in the bedroom and your Art in the kitchen, whatever suits you!

✔ Take a walk. Use the time to think about what you have learned that day.

Interpersonal intelligence

✔ Take part in a group activity like a sports club, drama group or debating club.

✔ Find a study buddy. Find another person to work with (this isn't always your best friend as you may be distracted chatting too much!).

✔ Use your phone and e-mail. This helps you to keep in touch with friends and family. You also learn to type more quickly and to communicate with abbreviated and coded words.

✔ Make time to talk to people you live with. Speak to them and ask how they are doing. This will improve relationships.

Intrapersonal intelligence

✔ Give yourself time. Take time for yourself. Look back on something you have done and ask yourself some questions – could you have done it better? Were you happy with the way it worked out?

✔ Read some self-improvement books. This will help you decide if you want to use any of the suggestions to get more out of life.

Emotional intelligence

Another type of intelligence is called **emotional intelligence**. This is about being **aware of other people** and their needs, as well as having your own feelings under control. Emotional intelligence is very important and a lot of people who end up doing well in life have this as a particular talent. You would expect a **responsible citizen** to be emotionally intelligent. Everyone can improve their emotional intelligence if they practise.

Make your brain work for you

When you're young, your brain is still developing. With a bit of effort, you can make it work even better. Try doing things differently and doing different things.

It's natural to have strengths and weaknesses. Remember to make the most of your strengths, but don't forget to improve your weaknesses with some of the exercises in this chapter. When you practise or try something new, your brain gets better at dealing with this information.

ACE Skills

This is a good time to be at school because nowadays we know so much more about the brain and how we can use it to learn efficiently. But for thousands of years wise people have known that it is important to *know yourself*. If you have some understanding of what makes *you* tick and what is the best way for *you* to learn, then *you* are likely to be a more successful learner. If you know how and when you function best, then you will make effective contributions in class and during extra-curricular activities. If you help others you will feel more confident within yourself and you will be acting very responsibly towards people round about you.

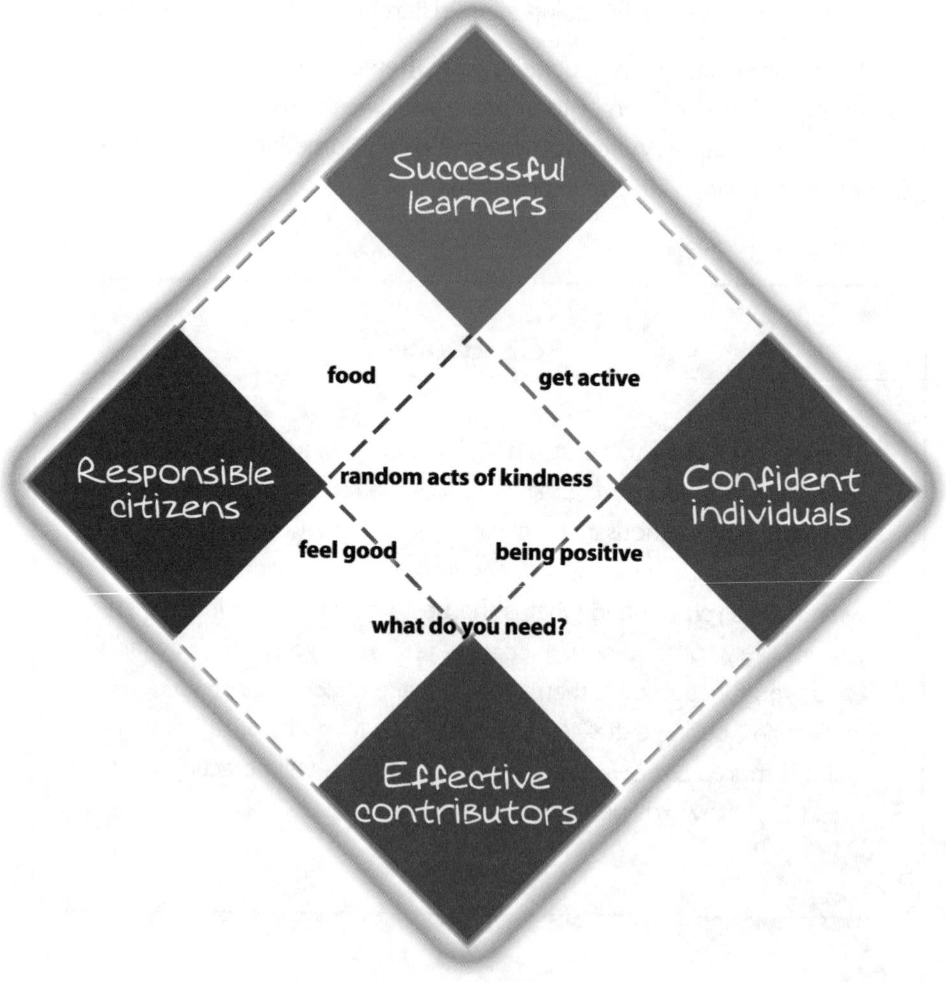

Successful learners

food

get active

Responsible citizens

random acts of kindness

Confident individuals

feel good

being positive

what do you need?

Effective contributors

Healthy lifestyles: eat well, get active and feel good

More and more people seem to be overweight, unfit and not particularly happy. Sadly, lots of young people are like this. But it doesn't have to be like this for you!

In this chapter you will learn how to look after yourself, physically and mentally. You will read about:

✔ **food** and how important it is that you eat well in order to live healthy lives

✔ **exercise** because that is just as important as food for good health

✔ **feeling good about yourself** which help with your mental health as well as physical health

✔ **random acts of kindness** because looking out for others is good for them and also good for you.

Looking after yourself isn't being selfish. It is the responsible thing to do. If you are healthy in mind and body you will, be able to learn more successfully because you brain will be in good shape and you'll be able to contribute effectively at sport and at work, be more confident and happy, because you will feel good about yourself.

What do you need?

We all need food and water – fuel – to survive, but you want to do more than just survive your life. You want to enjoy it. Fuel keeps our bodies working properly. Just as cars cannot go without their fuel, we need good quality, healthy food to keep us going. Food is our fuel.

Eating healthy foods is a great start to you feeling good. This chapter will give you the information you need to eat well and look after yourself properly.

Eating for your developing body

As you are growing up the amount of food you need and the type of food you eat changes. Your body is going through changes at this time and you need to make sure you feed it the correct nutrition.

As you go through adolescence, you might be more aware of your body and its needs. You will also realise that friends and people your own age are all growing and changing at different rates. This is also a time when you can feel clumsy – you might trip over nothing or stand on peoples' toes when you get up from the settee. You might also have a bit of puppy fat until you have grown into your body, and you might become spotty on your face, neck and back (severe cases are known as *acne*). Eating fresh fruit and vegetables that contain the essential nutrients for your skin will help at this time.

Looking after yourself with proper exercise and healthy food with all the nutrients you need can make a real difference to just about everything about your body. This will even help with your moods and how you get on at school. Moods can just come and go for no reason, so you need to know how to cope with them. Some foods will affect your moods more than others and it is a good idea to work out what foods you should avoid. For some people, foods with a lot of additives (the E numbers on the food labels) and high sugar content are not good and make their moods worse.

Be very careful that you do not fall into the trap of eating for comfort when you're unhappy. This can become a bad habit which is hard to give up once you start. Lots of adults regret starting comfort-eating when they were younger because they now have problems with their weight and eating patterns.

Eating for an amazing brain

It's important to follow a **balanced diet** to make sure your brain gets the fuel it needs. The food you eat when you're young will shape the way you grow up. Getting it right now will help you live a long healthy life. Getting it wrong can mean continuing illness and health problems.

To get the most from what you eat, you should choose a variety of foods from the five main food groups.

Group	Containing	
Fruit and vegetables	Vitamins and minerals	
Bread, cereals, pasta and potatoes	Carbohydrates	
Meat, fish, and alternatives	Protein	
Milk and dairy foods	Protein	
Foods containing fat, sugar and salt	Fat, sugar and salt	

The **Traffic Light System** will help you choose your diet sensibly if you are not too sure.

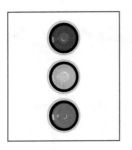

GREEN foods are good for you, and you can **GO** straight ahead and eat them.

AMBER foods are okay but you should **WAIT** or think before you choose or eat them.

RED foods can be bad for you if you eat too much and you should **STOP** and think about choosing or eating.

You should also drink about 6-8 glasses (1 litre) of liquid a day. This can be a combination of water, milk and fruit juice.

More about the food groups

Group 1: Fruit and **vegetables** provide **vitamins, minerals** and **dietary fibre**. The body cannot make many of the vitamins and minerals, so you need to get them in foods. You need these to help keep your body healthy and free from diseases. **GREEN TRAFFIC LIGHT**

Group 2: Bread, **cereals, pasta** and **potatoes** provide **carbohydrates**. Carbohydrates give your body energy to do things. There are two types of carbohydrates; **starch** (potatoes, rice, pasta and breads) and **sugar** (cakes, biscuits & sweets). Starch carbohydrates get a **GREEN** light, and sugar carbohydrates get an **AMBER** light.
GREEN TRAFFIC LIGHT / **AMBER TRAFFIC LIGHT**

Group 3: Meat, **fish** and **alternatives** provides **protein**. Protein is needed by the body for growth and repair purposes. The **AMBER** light is for fattier proteins like meat pies, some red meats, most nuts, processed meats, and fried processed protein foods like battered fish. The **GREEN** light is for lean or low fat proteins foods like chicken, turkey, white fish, quorn, & tofu.
AMBER TRAFFIC LIGHT / **GREEN TRAFFIC LIGHT**

Group 4: Milk and **dairy foods** provide **protein, calcium, phosphorous** and **vitamins**. Calcium and phosphorous help to make strong and healthy teeth and bones. Dairy foods often have a lot of fat hidden in them, so they get an

AMBER light. Try to eat the lower fat varieties of these foods. The **GREEN** light is for all the lower fat/light/reduced fat options.
AMBER TRAFFIC LIGHT / **GREEN TRAFFIC LIGHT**

Group 5: Foods containing **fat, sugar** provide **energy** to do activities. But the body only needs small amounts of fat and sugar, and a lot of foods have more than enough for your body. If fat is not used up in activities it is stored in the body for later. **Salt** is needed to keep the right amounts of body fluids, but too much salt can lead to high blood pressure. **RED TRAFFIC LIGHT**

What you need, where you get it and what it does for you		
Nutrient	Source – Where you get it	What is does for your body
Vitamin A	Carrots, fish, broccoli, cheese, eggs	Healthy eyes, hair and skin
Vitamin B	Granary and wholemeal breads, spinach, nuts, pulses	Healthy nerves and skin
Vitamin C	Oranges, kiwi fruit, green leafy vegetables, tomatoes, strawberries	Healthy gums, blood and skin Helps fight infection
Vitamin D	Eggs, milk, oily fish, dairy products	Healthy bones and teeth
Vitamin E	Nuts, avocados, tomatoes, green vegetables, wholemeal products	Healthy skin and cells
Calcium	Milk, green vegetables, white bread	Healthy teeth and bones
Iron	Red meats, eggs, watercress, nuts, mangoes, kidney beans	Healthy blood
Phosphorous	Milk and cheese	Healthy teeth and bones
Protein (animal)	Milk, meat, fish, eggs, cheese	Healthy growth and repair of the body
Protein (non-animal)	Soya and rice milk, cheeses, nuts, pulses, vegetables	Healthy growth and repair of the body
Carbohydrate (starch)	Rice, pasta, potatoes, cereals, breads, pulses	Energy for the body
Carbohydrate (sugar)	Cakes, biscuits, pastries, puddings, sweets	Energy for the body
Fat	Most processed foods especially fast foods. Chocolate, chips, crisps nuts, butter, margarines, oils	Energy for the body

Healthy lifestyles

Using up your fuel

The table below will help you to understand that what you eat is your fuel, and you have to use it up or you will store it as fat. The table shows how far you have to walk to work off the calories of some fast foods. You can of course dance it off, play football, or go swimming. But if you do not use up all this energy, the body stores it for later – in the form of fat.

Fast foods	Calories	Hours to walk	Distance
Kentucky Fried Chicken Original Chicken Salad	400	1.8 hours	5.5 miles
Burger King Chicken BLT Baguette and Large Coke	785	3.5 hours	10.5 miles
Big Mac, Medium Fries and Small Vanilla Milkshake	1200	5.5 hours	16.5 miles
Pizza Hut Individual Margherita Pan Pizza and Garlic Bread	1300	6 hours	18 miles

If you eat a lot of takeaways like the ones in the table, you could be storing up lots of trouble. At the very least, you could be heading towards being spotty, overweight *and* having bad teeth!

Your health is partly your responsibility, so be positive and proud about it. Eating the correct foods and exercising will ensure your body and brain work at their peak performance.

Snacking

Young people who are going through a growth spurt and who are energetic during the day may become hungry between meals. This hunger leads to snacking. As long as the snacks you eat are from the green or maybe a little portion from the amber food groups, you will be all right. If you snack on junk foods which are high in fat, salt or sugar (red food groups), then you may well have health problems later on in your life. If you eat lots of junk food snacks and don't exercise, you're almost certainly storing up trouble for yourself.

You need to be careful about snacks. It's easy to think of a Mars Bar as a simple snack to eat between meals, but a standard Mars Bar has 284 calories in it. That means you need to walk for over an hour to use it up! Similarly, a Snickers bar has 319 calories and a bag of crisps has 183 calories. Better snacks would be an apple, which only has 53 calories, or a portion of grapes, which has about 20 calories. Apples and grapes also have lots of good vitamins for your body.

Snacking can be sensible. If you choose light bites like sandwiches made from pitta, tortillas, wholemeal breads, fruits, raw vegetables, nuts and raisins, you'll be making better choices for your health.

Moods and memory

What you eat and the way you use your food as fuel can affect everything about your body and brain. You can make a difference to your health by making the right choices.

What you eat can affect your moods and memory. Foods that are slower to digest take blood away from the brain and therefore reduce your ability to think. There are some foods, like tuna, which help you keep mentally alert because some of the chemicals in fish help the brain to function more efficiently.

Get active!

You need to exercise to keep your body fit and strong. Regular exercise helps tone all the body's muscles, including the heart. If you work your body, it will be in better condition and you will feel healthier and have more energy. Fitness is an important part of being healthy. It may also help you feel more confident and happy in yourself.

Exercise pumps up the brain as well as the body. So regular exercise will help you to be more:

- ✔ focussed
- ✔ energetic
- ✔ self-confident
- ✔ brain-powered
- ✔ fun to be with.

Not everyone wants to exercise and it might be a real challenge for you to get involved. There are lots of exercise activities you could take up and it might be a good idea to try a few first to see which you like best. A good way to do this is to go along to taster sessions at local clubs, sports centres or extra-curricular sports at school.

You'll probably find that your enjoyment increases as you get more involved with an activity. You might not want to exercise with other people, especially if you are feeling uncomfortable with your body shape or know you are not too coordinated! If this is the case, try something at home with an exercise or dance DVD.

There are also plenty of sports or exercises you can do on your own, like cycling, swimming, walking, horse riding and running.

If you prefer company try a sport or activity that involves being with other people like football, rugby, volleyball, basketball or hockey or join an aerobics or gymnastics class.

How much exercise should you aim for?

Without realising it, you're probably getting some exercise during the day. If you do an **hour of aerobic activity** that works the heart and lungs (walking your dog, cycling, swimming, and dancing) every day, you'll be getting enough exercise.

If you don't get that much exercise just in your normal activities, you need to make a bit more effort. Find an activity that is fun and you can do with friends. You should be trying to get an hour of exercise every day, but if you can't manage that, you should try to do as much as you can. Don't give up before you've even started!

Feel good, be confident, be happy

To get the most from life, you have to learn to think **positively**! As well as eating properly and taking enough exercise, you can make your life better by practising feeling good. This means you have to think about yourself and the way you live your life.

One way to get to know yourself better is to try to think about the different people you meet and mix with. Think about:

- ✔ what you like about them/don't like?
- ✔ what makes them interesting/not interesting?
- ✔ what motivates (makes them tick) them /doesn't motivate them?
- ✔ what are their personal needs?
- ✔ what do they do for you?

Thinking about these questions will tell a lot about yourself and what it is that makes you happy.

Happiness

This book is about helping you to do well in your studies. If you are happy, you **will** do better at school. If you are unhappy (at home, at school or with your friends), you will probably find studying very difficult. So, what is happiness and what can we do to make ourselves feel happier?

Some children and adults learn to be unhappy or helpless. They tell themselves that they cannot do things and that their life cannot be any better. They don't believe anything can improve their lives. This may be because they are frightened to try in case they fail.

But you **can** learn to be happier, optimistic and more positive about life. Happy optimistic people tend to live longer and healthier lives. They concentrate on the things they are good at – their strengths – and do not allow themselves to get depressed about what they are not so good at.

Of course, you should try hard to do better at things you need to improve, but you don't do that by telling yourself that you are no good. You need to be positive about yourself. Never forget that you have your own particular strengths. That should please you and make you more optimistic about what you can achieve when you tackle the things that find harder.

What makes you happy?

We all have different things that make us happy, but these different things fit into certain key categories:

- ✔ family relationships
- ✔ work
- ✔ friends and community
- ✔ health
- ✔ money

Let's look at some of these and see how they might affect your studying.

Family relationships

You spend a lot of time with your family, and the way you get on with your parents and your brothers and sisters will have a big effect on your happiness.

Positive affect on your happiness if:	Negative affect on your happiness if:
your parents get on together	your parents don't get on together
you are able to talk through problems	people argue in the house
there is no pressure put on you to achieve	too much pressure is put on you to achieve
the family takes an interest in you	the family does not take an interest in you

If you can identify with some of the negatives, then you must try to do something to make things better. It may mean sitting down and calmly telling someone how you feel. This may be difficult for you and you may want to ask someone to help you, like a teacher or a family relative.

Work

Your work right now is going to school. It is really important to feel safe, secure and happy at school. The best way of being happy at school is to try to play a full part in daily school life. School can give you great opportunities, and the more effort you make to have a good time, the more likely it is that you'll enjoy yourself and become a **successful learner** and a **confident individual**.

However, things don't always go to plan, and one thing that can take your confidence away is **bullying**. We asked a group of 12 year olds to describe what bullying meant to them. Here are some of their responses:

I think bullying can be very upsetting for someone and it can hurt them emotionally and sometimes people can get hurt physically. I think that the most upsetting bullying is when someone gets bullied and laughed at by a group of people.   **Jenny**

I think bullying is silly and very hurtful, I've never been bullied but I know I would never want to be because it is horrible.   **Nula**

I think bullying is horrible. I was bullied and I told my mum who phoned the teacher and it stopped. I then started to bully, I don't know why and I feel bad I did. My mum explained how sad I had been and probably how sad the person I was bullying was, so I stopped. Since then I have started to control my temper and keep control of myself.   **Kieran**

If you are being bullied, you must tell someone. Talk to a teacher or a friend or your parent. Remember it's not you who is in the wrong but the person or people who are doing the bullying. Like in Kieran's description above, you often find that a bully has been bullied themselves. It is not normal behaviour to want to be a bully and bullies are often weak and vulnerable people who do not realise just how much pain they have caused to their victim.

www.leckieandleckie.co.uk

If you're having problems with bullying, you can find the addresses of some useful websites on the ACE Study Skills page in the Leckie & Leckie Learning Lab.

Friends and community

Friends matter a lot. People are happy when they have friends to talk to and hang out with. It is also important to respect your wider community (neighbours and surroundings). Try to get along with people and help them out when you can.

So, what do you do if you do not have friends?

Get out of the house! Look back at the section on being active in this chapter. It might take a bit of courage but go and join a club. It could be a football or swimming club, the Scouts, Guides or Cadets or a war-gaming club, bird watching or a drama club; it could be kickboxing, badminton, gymnastics; or it might be a band. Whatever it is, get out and meet people who have similar interests to you. And if you do not have any interests, get some! Life is too short and the world is too wonderful for you to sit around saying you are bored and that you have no friends.

Here's another good idea. **Switch off the television!** Watching too much of it is a great way *not* to meet friends. Cut your viewing by half and see the rewards!

Random Acts of Kindness – go on surprise yourself!

Trying to think about other people (and your pets!) instead of yourself can help you to be a better friend or family member. It also gives you responsibility to care and show you can make people or your pets feel comfortable and enjoy being with you. You'll feel more confident and you'll probably be more popular!

Have you ever thought of doing something helpful in your community, like volunteering for a litter clear-up or going messages for an older person? Does that sound a bit sappy? It isn't. Helping other people will make you a happier person, quite apart from the good you will doing for others. Random Acts of Kindness (RAKs) are a great way to make yourself feel good. You could practice a RAK a day. Here are some suggestions:

✔ Phone a grandparent or an elderly relative and ask how they are.

✔ Tidy up in the house without being asked.

✔ Pick some flowers and give them to someone who is feeling low.

✔ Do a good turn for somebody.

✔ Write a letter to someone.

✔ Volunteer to help out in the community.

Ask yourself: 'What do other people think about me? Do they think I am kind and helpful?' If the answer is 'No', then try to do something about it. And then try to behave in a way that ensures they *do* see you as a kind person. If you do, they will be happier … and so will you.

Health

If your health is making you unhappy, you need to do something about it.

✔ If a medical problem is worrying you, **talk to someone** and go and see the doctor or the school nurse.
✔ If you are unfit, **start taking exercise**. Don't just think about it – do it!
✔ If your diet is bad, change it or suggest to your parents and family to try to **change your diet** and then do it – together.

All this is much easier to write about than to do. It can be embarrassing going to the doctor. When you are not sporty, or when you are very unfit, exercise can be quite painful. You worry you might get laughed at. And as for eating properly, junk food is designed to be tasty and addictive and giving it up is very difficult. All very true. But … you still must try to do the right thing. And when you do make the effort, you'll soon find out how much better you feel.

Money

Money doesn't always make you happy. If you are poor, getting more money immediately makes you happier. But, if you are reasonably well-off – and that does not mean having a lot of money, just having enough to live on – then getting more money does not bring more happiness.

Having a lot of stuff doesn't make you happier either, or at least not for long. You might think you absolutely must have a new iPod to be happy, but, although getting it will make you feel better for a short while, this feeling will very quickly wear off (remember your Christmas list!). There will be something else soon enough that you think you must have. We all know it's nice to get things, but this is not the secret of either happiness or success at school.

Being sensible about happiness and acting positively

Reading about all the things that affect your happiness may have been making you unhappy! Why me, you might be thinking? Why do things keep going wrong for me? Why are other people happier than me?

It is perfectly natural to have such thoughts, to look at other people and think that they are doing better than you. But it is important that you do not get into the habit of being jealous of others. You can never know what other people are thinking. You cannot measure their happiness. If you could, you might be surprised.

It is a very unusual person who does not find their mood changes frequently. No one can be happy all the time. Life is full of challenges and no one can escape hard times when things do not go smoothly. There is always something that does not work out quite the way we want it to, from our football team not winning, to a friend letting us down, or getting a poor mark in an exam.

But then there are the *really* hard times, like when someone we love dies or when we lose a pet or when we get badly hurt. The truth is that life *is* tough at times and we all have to be sensible in the way we look at our life. When we're on a bit of a downer, we should still try our best; when things are great and we feel very happy, we shouldn't get too carried away. Neither situation will last forever. They are part of being alive. What we should always try to do is **learn from experience** and keep moving forward in our lives.

Take control!

There are some things which you can't do anything about. But, there are other things which make you unhappy which you *have* to do something about.

If things are bothering you, like your school work being too difficult, or if you're being bullied or if you're not getting on with a teacher, you need to do something to sort the problem. If you don't, it will affect your performance in school. Always **share your problems** with someone you can trust. Talk to your parent, teacher, friend or phone a help-line. The other person may not know the answer or fully understand your problem, but you will not be alone in looking for a solution. You must not just shrug our shoulders and try to put up with things.

It's your life and you should be in charge of it.

ACE Skills

Your body is yours for as long as you live! You can change a phone and you can buy a new computer, but you cannot replace your body. The good news is that if you take care of it, your body will last far longer than any phone or computer. Feed and exercise your body, look after it with pride, and you will learn successfully and be a more confident individual. The healthier you are the happier you will be, and the more able you will be to make an effective contribution to your school and community. The body you have now is the only body you are going to have. Caring for it and not abusing it is surely the responsible thing to do. Why choose to be negative about things when by being positive you can get so much more out of life and feel so much better about yourself?

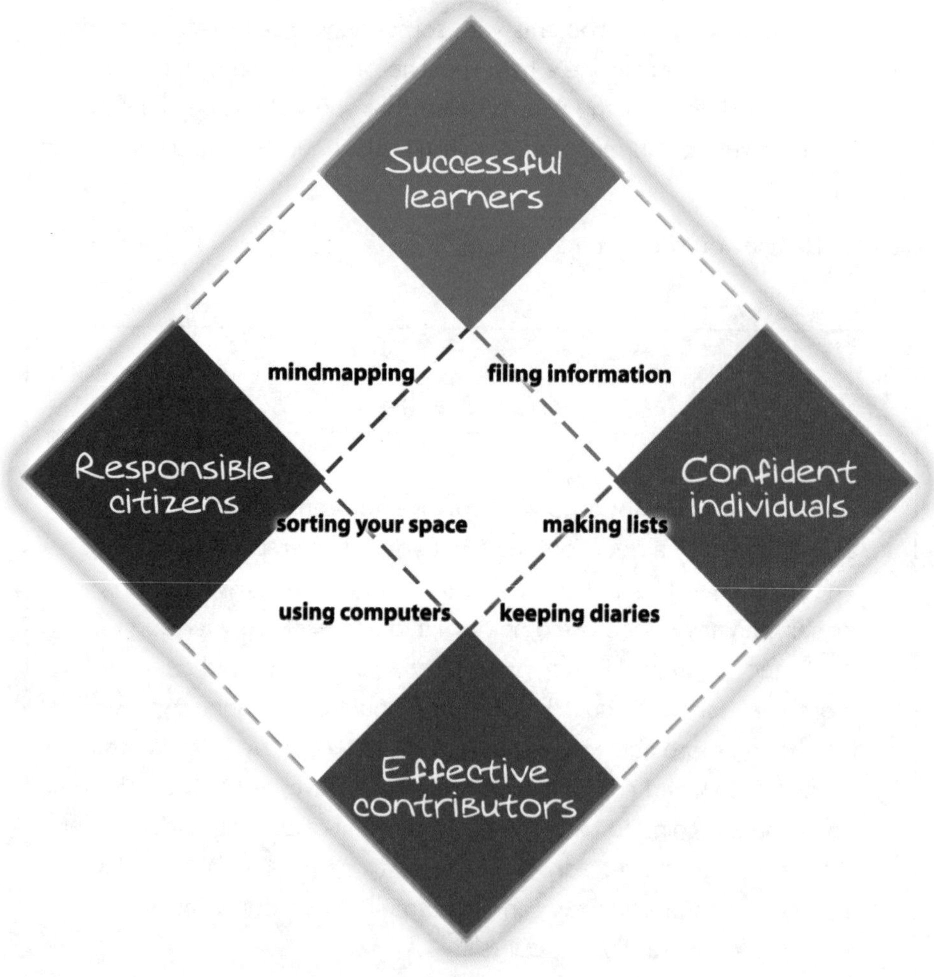

Successful
learners

mindmapping   filing information

Responsible
citizens

sorting your space   making lists

Confident
individuals

using computers   keeping diaries

Effective
contributors

Getting organised

This chapter is about ways to organise yourself so that you can learn more efficiently at school and get more out of life generally. You will read about:

- ✔ diaries which tell you of what you have to do in the future
- ✔ mindmaps which are a very good way of collecting your thoughts and remembering key information
- ✔ sorting your space and filing information which will help you find things quickly, study more efficiently and help you feel in control of things
- ✔ keeping lists which is good fun to do anyway but will also prepare you for more detailed note-taking when you are older
- ✔ using your computer efficiently so you can keep all your files organised.

Getting organised will help you feel **more confident** about yourself. It will help you learn more **successfully**, be able to make better **contributions** better, and have a **responsible approach** to anything you do.

Getting organised

Why get organised?

Getting organised means you can make the most of your time. Learn a few simple techniques and good habits now and it will be good for you at school, at home and in the future.

Some people seem to thrive on chaos. Things may look a mess but just in time they can always find what they want. Most of us, however, get very anxious when we can't something we're looking for or when we're running late. We feel better when we know that everything is where it should be and that we are in control of our lives. Good organisation can help us feel more confident, make us more effective and help us to study more successfully.

Being well organised helps you achieve more at school and in your own leisure time. You'll be amazed at how much more control you can have over your life.

Keeping a diary

Diaries can do two things. You can use them for planning what you are going to do in the future and they can tell you what you did in the past. Let's concentrate first on the future.

It is easy to forget appointments – when you've got to go to the dentist, when a piece of homework is due or when it's a friend's birthday. Just now perhaps a parent keeps you right or maybe you feel you can remember everything, but as you get older you will find that the number of really important things you must not forget will get bigger. You need a diary and the sooner you get into the way of using one the better.

You can buy your own diary, but many schools give their pupils fancy versions called planners. They are all much the same and the pages will look something like the one printed here.

Sunday	Thursday
	Environmental Studies project due
Monday Dad's Birthday	**Friday** Football training
Tuesday	**Saturday**
Wednesday	**Notes** Get Dad a Birthday present

This page is a bit too simple. Adding a bit more detail will make your diary much more useful. The next example was made by a secondary school pupil.

Sunday	Thursday
Morning Afternoon Evening	Reg 1 2 Int 3 Environmental Studies project due 4 Lunch 5 6 After Evening

Monday	Friday
Reg 1 Maths homework due 2 Int 3 4 Lunch 5 6 After Evening	Reg 1 2 Int Meeting in room 8 about ski trip 3 4 Lunch 5 6 After Evening football training at 6.30

Tuesday	Saturday
Reg 1 2 Int 3 History test 4 Lunch 5 6 After Evening	Morning Afternoon Evening

Wednesday	Notes
Reg 1 2 Int 3 4 Lunch 5 6 After Evening	1. Buy Dad a birthday present 2. Buy new shin guards 3. 4. 5.

You can see there are six periods in the day and clubs can have meetings at interval, lunchtime and after school.

Quickly writing in the periods and breaks means you can make the diary much more precise and helpful. The Notes section at the bottom has been made into a To Do list where you can list the things you have to do that week (and get satisfaction when you cross them off).

Planning with your diary

The point of keeping a diary is to know what is going to happen in the future and to plan accordingly. If you know that there is a History test on Tuesday, then you should be revising for it in the days before. Perhaps you should write in previous Sunday *revise for History test next Tuesday*. This is a good example of being organised. Look ahead and do your revision in good time and you won't panic on the day of the test and you'll feel more confident about doing well.

Your school may give you a diary or planner. It will be full of useful information. Listen carefully to the advice your teacher gives you on how to use it. But you should still be able to adapt it to suit yourself.

If you want a diary that is really different, you could use a mindmap. (You can read about mindmaps on page 46.) In the middle is the weekly date, the main branches are the days of the week, and the sub-branches are the appointments, homeworks and activities that you have to remember. It might also have a list of targets or things to do. It could look something like this:

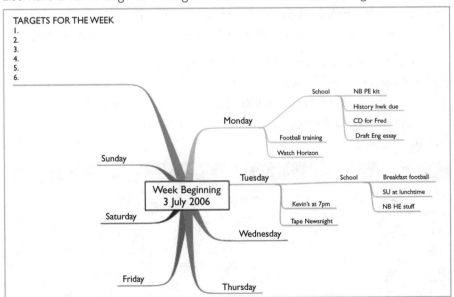

TARGETS FOR THE WEEK
1.
2.
3.
4.
5.
6.

Sunday

Monday — School — NB PE kit / History hwk due / CD for Fred / Draft Eng essay
Football training
Watch Horizon

Week Beginning 3 July 2006

Tuesday — School — Breakfast football / SU at lunchtime / NB HE stuff
Kevin's at 7pm
Tape Newsnight

Saturday

Wednesday

Friday

Thursday

Getting organised

Your diary is history!

The second reason for keeping a diary is to record things that have already happened. At the end of the day, or week, you can write into your diary all the various things you did, or heard or said, people you met, places you visited, and so on. Keeping a diary sometimes makes you feel better about yourself, and it's a good way of making sure you don't forget things you've enjoyed doing. Some old diaries have become important historical documents.

www.leckieandleckie.co.uk

To see some whole class activities and examples of historical diaries, visit the ACE Study Skills pages on the Leckie & Leckie Learning Lab website and read the Diaries download.

Drawing mindmaps

Mindmaps are a very good way of organising key information, making it easier to remember the most important facts. Drawing a mindmap also helps you *understand* a difficult topic. Mindmaps are a different way of organising information, so you need to spend a bit of time learning how to draw them.

Usually people make notes in what we call a *linear* way. The five aspects of personal organisation, in the box at the start of this chapter, are printed in a linear way. The table below is another example. It is a simple table showing the capital cities and the populations of the six countries which began the European Union.

Country	Population (millions)	Capital
France	62.9	Paris
Germany	83.2	Berlin
Belgium	10.2	Brussels
Italy	57.7	Rome
Netherlands	16.3	The Hague
Luxembourg	0.5	Luxembourg City

If you are more left-brained you may like this linear format. If you're more right-brained, you might find mindmaps a better way of organising information. In a mindmap, the key idea is placed at the centre of the page and all the related information spreads out in all directions, like the branches and twigs of a tree.

In a mindmap the European Union information would look like this:

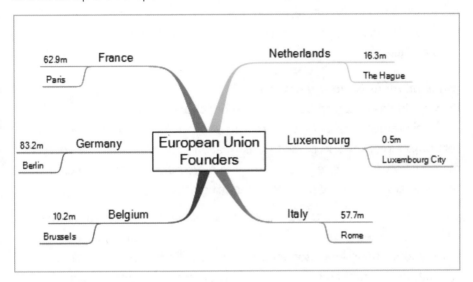

Look at the different parts of the diagram:

1   The title is in the middle, in large letters.
2   The six founder countries form the main branches, in slightly smaller letters.
3   The population information and the capital cities are on sub-branches, or twigs, in lettering which is smaller still.
4   Each branch, with its sub-branches, is a different colour. This is because the brain finds colour helpful when it is trying to remember information.

This mindmap was drawn using a computer programme, but it is just as easy to draw mindmaps using coloured pencils and a blank sheet of paper.

Draw your own mindmap

Do your own version of the above mindmap. Make the branches as wavy as you like and use plenty of colour. Then give it to someone to test you. See if you can remember all the information.

If you've enjoyed drawing the mindmap, then you will have learned important information at the same time (probably without even realising it!). To remember these facts again in the future, picture the mindmap in your head, see the branches and the colours, and then you will see the countries, populations and cities as well.

Make mindmaps more memorable!

How could this mindmap be made even better and even more memorable? The brain remembers pictures, so mindmaps work well because they are a sort of picture. They also break the information into easy chunks for your memory. So why not give your brain some more help, and have some fun at the same time, by adding pictures to the mindmap.

One easy way of adding to the mindmaps would be to add the flags of the different countries (you can find the flags on the internet or drawn from a book). Notice how similar some of the flags are. But the mind map links the flag with the country **and** the colour of the branch. This stops you getting

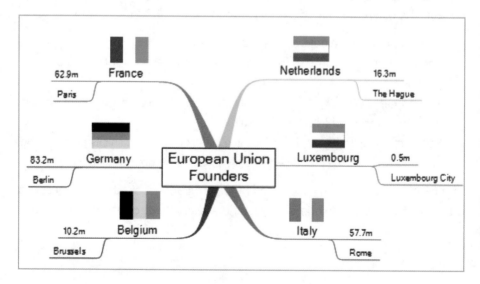

mixed up. Alternatively, for France, you could add something that is associated with France, like a picture of the Eiffel Tower or a French baguette. Then do the same for the other countries (you could have a picture of the Coliseum or a pizza for Italy).

We now have a colourful, memorable picture, packed with information, which has been enjoyable to create. Mindmaps help you get organised – planning, recording, remembering – and they also assist with understanding. You do, though, have to practise to get the best out of them.

The best mindmaps are the ones you do yourself. They can be as simple or as elaborate as you want to make them. Try them and find out if they work for you.

Here are mindmaps for an imaginary school. The first is quite basic, just showing branches for some of the main features of the school. The second mindmap is more useful, giving you a full list of the teachers and assistants at the school. Copy the first mindmap and add branches so it describes your school. You can add details to say what the assembly hall is used for, the number of classrooms, the games played in the playground, the staff who work in the school office and so on.

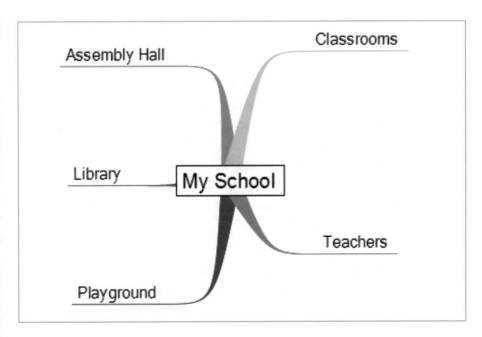

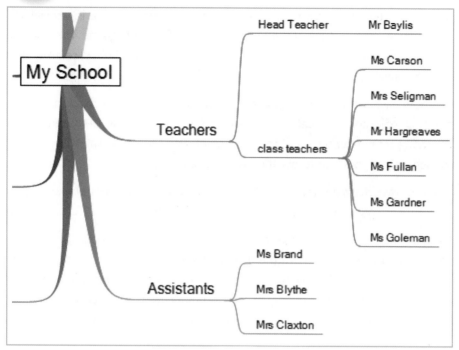

More mindmaps

Now try drawing some other mindmaps. You will be able to think of subjects for yourself, but here are some suggestions:

✔ *my family* (parents, grandparents, brothers and sisters, their names, their ages – if they tell you – their jobs, their interests)

✔ *my town* (population, main employment, interesting sights, big shops)

✔ *my favourite sports* (a branch for each sport and then sub-branches for more information about where you play, what level you are at)

✔ *my favourite pop star* (age, best songs, girl/boyfriend, appearance)

✔ *my friends* (name each and say a bit about their interests)

✔ *my favourite film* (branches could include the stars, the most exciting moments, the main locations).

Remember to use colour and pictures, if you can. You could stick photographs of your family on the mindmap. Try not to write too much on each branch. Actually one word is best. If you want to add more information, create extra sub-branches.

Sorting your space

Everyone needs a bit of space that is just theirs. At the moment you might have your own room or you might be sharing with brothers or sisters.

Even if you only have a very small space to yourself, keeping it tidy will help you:

✔ feel better about yourself
✔ be ready for school
✔ make better use of our time.

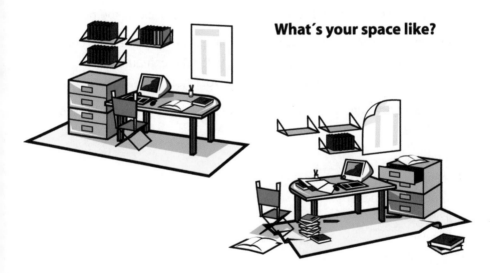

What's your space like?

So, look around your space, whatever it is. Could it be used better? There are a few things you could do to make better use of the room you have:

✔ make your bed
✔ fold or hang up your clothes
✔ stack books, magazines, folders, school jotters neatly in a bookcase or on a shelf
✔ get rid of obvious rubbish – empty bottles, dirty mugs, waste paper
✔ give the room a vacuum, sweep or dust.

Getting organised

Quite easy, so far! But now have a look at all your stuff. Are there a few things that are not exactly rubbish, but that you know you don't really need. So, throw away the things that are just taking up space (or see if anyone else wants them before you throw them out).

Look around your room or space again. Does it look better? Do you feel quite pleased with yourself? Of course you do, so decide immediately that you are going to keep it this way … and get pleasure out of doing so.

Getting ready for school

Let's think about what you need for doing well at school. Having a bookcase, a desk and your own computer is great. But you can make do with a shelf for your folders and books, and you can write at another table in the house.

Wherever you sit to write or read, try to make sure you have a decent light and that you are not in your own shadow. As for the computer, you can use one in the school if you do not have one in your house.

Apart from books and notes, what are the tools for the job? Your 'toolbox' should have:

- ✔ pens
- ✔ pencils
- ✔ a pencil sharpener
- ✔ rubbers
- ✔ a ruler
- ✔ a calculator

It helps to keep everything together in the same place so you know exactly where it all is. Try to replace anything that gets worn out or lost. If you can afford it, try to have two sets of everything, one for home and one for school. Keep your school set in a pencil case. Your home set should be in a desk drawer or in a box.

School books and folders should be kept together as well. They can be stacked in a bookcase or on a shelf along with your toolbox. Jotters may have to be laid flat because they do not stand so easily. They should be labelled clearly.

All this is very easy. In fact, it is so obvious that you wonder why people allow themselves to get into a mess. But they do! Once you have got yourself organised, you must be very determined to stay that way. Put things back in the right place and don't let other people mess up your system. Take pride and pleasure in being efficient.

Getting your space or room properly organised is an example of a good habit which, if you get it right, will really help you in the future. But it will be also be good for you *now*. It will help you do well at school; you will feel proud of *your* space; and you will not waste time looking for things.

Using folders and ring binders

Folders and ring binders are very useful for keeping notes filed in an organised way, so it's easy to use to find the notes when you're learning them for exams. Some people find it hard to look after folders and ring binders properly, so it's a good idea to learn a few basic rules.

The first thing to think about is: how many ring binders do you need? One binder might be enough at primary school, especially if it is a big one able to hold a lot of notes. In secondary school, you might have to have one for every subject. If that is the case, you will have a problem carrying a lot of folders back and forward every day (unless you are lucky enough to have use of a locker at school). The answer might be to keep your subject folders at home, unless you need one of them on a particular day, and just have the one folder – a *daily folder* – which you keep with you in the school. It should contain only the notes you are using at the moment in each class. This system can work well, but only if you are very careful to take out each night the notes you are now finished with, putting them into their own subject folder, and topping up the daily binder with the notes you will need for the following day.

If you are using ring binders, there are certain golden rules:

- ✔ label them clearly on the spine so you know exactly what they contain
- ✔ make sure all the notes are punched and in the rings. It's really annoying when unpunched notes keep falling out of a ring binder
- ✔ use dividers to organise the notes into sections
- ✔ file the notes as soon as you get them, in the right section. That way you'll find them again easily
- ✔ don't keep notes that are out of date or torn and difficult to read. Get replacement copies if necessary
- ✔ make sure they can stand properly in a bookcase or stack them in a cardboard or plastic box. If you don't do this they will fall over, slide off the shelf, spill their notes and really make you fed up.

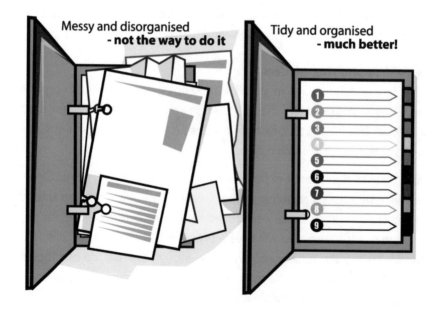

**Messy and disorganised
- not the way to do it**

**Tidy and organised
- much better!**

Collecting key information

In a few years time, you will be sitting Standard Grade and Higher exams. After that, you may go on to college and university. To be successful you will have to learn to take notes from lectures and from books. A lot of students struggle because they never learn this skill. When the time comes, you should try hard to develop your skills at note-taking. There are some good books which can help you – have a look in your school library for *Study Skills and Strategies* by McInally and Summers.

Making lists

You don't have to worry about taking notes at the moment, but you can start thinking about the ways you can collect information. A good way to get started is to get into the habit of making lists.

People love lists. Look at all the TV programmes there have been about the top hundred of this and the top hundred of that, the best comedy programmes, the best adverts, the scariest films, the greatest World Cup goals. We like to know who is in the Charts and what the number one is. You probably discuss with your friends who your favourite singers, actors and sportsmen and women are. You can use this very natural behaviour to help you collect key information.

An easy starting point is to list the music you own and how much you like each track. iTunes is a popular piece of computer software which does this for you. Look at this picture taken from iTunes:

	Name	Time	Artist	Album	Genre ▲	My Rating
1	☑ In competition for the worst time	2:42	Idlewild	Make Another World	Alternative	★★
2	☑ Too Many DJs	3:28	Soulwax	Too Many DJ's	Alternative	★★★★
3	☑ Rahaye Rahaye	14:19	Safri Boys	Bhangra Fever	Bhangra	★★★★
4	☑ Getting Away With It	4:23	The Egg	Travelator	Electronic	★★★★★
5	☑ C'mon Cincinnati	3:54	Delakota	C'mon Cincinnati	Electronica	★★★
6	☑ Shake Ur Body	3:17	Di/Shy FX/T.Power	Cream Anthems	Electronica	★★★★
7	☑ The Thin Line	3:02	Skeewiff	Bounce	Electronica	★★★★
8	☑ Ready to Go	5:01	Republica	Republica	Pop	★★
9	☑ Dusty	2:53	Astrid	Strange Weather Lately	Rock	★
10	☑ Whatever Happened to My Ro...	4:37	Black Rebel Motorcycle Club	B.R.M.C.	Rock	★★
11	☑ Test Transmission	9:50	Kasabian	Kasabian	Rock	★★
12	☑ Hip Bounce	4:31	Scuba Z	The Vanishing American Family	Rock	★★★★
13	☑ Not the Children of God	5:07	Spec X-Ray	Bounce	Techno	★★★

Getting organised

The list shows the names of the pieces of music, the time that each lasts, the artist, the album and the genre. But the last column is the fun bit. iTunes lets you give your own rating to the piece of music. You can give it anything from 1 to 5 stars according to how you feel about it.

Of course, you don't need iTunes for this list. You could very easily draw a table in a notebook and write in the same information. The important bit is the star rating because you are actually deciding what your own opinion is on the music.

Thinking for yourself, making up your own mind on music, or anything else, is very important. It is right to listen to people who know more than you. You can always learn from experts. You should try to hear different points of view. But then it is good to work out your own opinion. In fact, your list would be even better if it had a space after the star rating for you to write a sentence on why you have chosen the number of stars that you did. You could easily include such a space if you drew your own music table. You could make similar lists for your books as well as your music.

When you finish reading a book, you should add it to your list.

Date	Author	Title	Rating	Comment
23 May 2007	J K Rowling	Harry Potter and the Philosopher's Stone	*****	Really like this. Good story and quite scary in bits.
6 July 2007	McInally and Summers	Study Skills and Strategies	*****	Brilliant book. Must tell the Headteacher to order lots for the school.

In the Date column, record when you *finished* the book. You must not cheat on yourself. It's easy to note a book which you've just started ... but then never finish.

The Rating column lets you record your opinion again and the final column gives you a space to say, very briefly, what you think.

Keeping a reading list is a bit like your diary. Imagine being able to look back in five years' time and reminding yourself not only of the books you have read, but what you thought about them at the time. Your opinion may have changed.

The list can also motivate you to read more. Why not set yourself a target to read 12 books in the year – a book a month. Think how pleased you will feel if, by Hogmanay, you have 12 or more books on the list. Without realising it, you will also have helped prepare yourself for studying and work in later life. You can always put *this* book down as the first on your list.

Here are another couple of lists you might like to try keeping. They tie in with the earlier chapters in the book and maintaining them will motivate you to keep eating and exercising well.

What I ate this week (be honest!)						
	Breakfast	In between	Lunch	In between	Tea	After tea
Sunday						
Monday						
Tuesday						
Wednesday						
Thursday						
Friday						
Saturday						

Healthy eating rating for the week (put a X on the line to show how you did):

Healthy   **Unhealthy**

Exercise I took this week					
	Morning	Lunchtime	Afternoon	After school	Evening
Sunday					
Monday					
Tuesday					
Wednesday					
Thursday					
Friday					Football training (120 mins) ***
Saturday					

Exercise rating for the week (put a X on the line to show how you did):

Healthy   **Unhealthy**

For the exercise list include walking or cycling to school, PE classes, training and games. Put a time in minutes against each bit of exercise. You could also give it a star rating according to how energetic it was, as in the football training example.

Lists are fun to keep. You can add them to your diary and they tell you a lot about yourself. They'll also keep you organised and motivate you to do better. They will prepare you for proper note-taking when you are older. Remember also that they don't just have to be about yourself. They could list information about famous people, football teams, capital cities, historical dates and so on.

It's interesting that a lot of famous people kept notes, recording their thoughts, keeping their special lists, drawing their mindmaps/diagrams. Perhaps you could learn from them.

www.leckieandleckie.co.uk
To see some examples of historical notes and lists, visit
the Leckie & Leckie Learning Lab and read the Journals download.

Blogging

Another good way of recording what you think about things is by *blogging* on the internet. Blogs are online journals and thousands of people are writing them. They're a great way of sharing your ideas with people all over the world. But be careful if you read other people's blogs – some of them are excellent, and well worth reading, but others are a complete waste of time.

Using your computer

A computer can be very helpful to get you organised. They are a great way of storing and presenting information in ways that will make your studies more effective. Written work that has been word processed or converted into a presentation with pictures can look really good. But the computer can also be used to:

✔ organise and store information
✔ investigate and research on the internet
✔ communicate with other people who have similar interests to you.

However, you need to keep it tidy if you're going to make the best of it.

Organising and storing information

When you switch on your computer the first screen you see is the desktop. Like a proper desk, it should be well organised so you can find what you want quickly and easily. If you use your computer a lot, you'll quickly create a lot of documents, and it's important to keep them organised in folders.

Just as with paper in ring binders, you must file electronic documents in the proper place. Your computer probably already has a folder caller *My Documents*, and you can create lots of other folders in this big folder. It's a good idea to have separate folders for all your school subjects, and you can also have other folders for your other interests.

Whenever you start a new document, you should name it clearly and store it in the right folder. If it's a document you are working on over a few days, you can put a temporary shortcut on the desktop for convenience so it's easy to find and open when you want it. Remember to get rid of the shortcut when you move on to something else.

This diagram shows how a secondary pupil, who tries to do most of her homework on her computer, has got things sorted out very well.

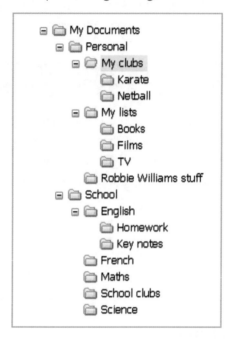

Inside *My Documents* she has created two folders called *School* and *Personal*. Everything to do with school goes into the *School* folder and everything else goes into the *Personal*.

Within the *School* folder, she has created a folder for four subjects, but it could have been a lot more. If you study twelve subjects, you should probably have twelve folders. In each subject folder, there are two further folders, one for *Key Notes* and one for *Homework*. In the *Key Notes* are all the things she has found out about the subject, the information she will have to learn up eventually for exams. In the *Homework* folder is the stuff she has to work on at the moment. In the diagram above, the *Key Notes* and the *Homework* folders are shown for *English* but, of course, she has *Key Notes* and *Homework* folders for every subject.

There is a folder for *School Clubs* where she can keep information about her extra-curricular activities.

In the *Personal* section of the diagram, you can see there are folders for her *Lists*, for her *Clubs* and for pictures and stories about *Robbie Williams*. You will have different interests and information that you want to store, so you will want to create different folders. But whatever documents you have, you'll always need to keep them organised.

Naming documents

You can make life much easier for yourself if you save documents with names which tell you what the document is about. For example, if you've got to write an *essay* about your *holidays* for your *English homework*, you could use the name *Enghwk-myholsessay*. It might be even more helpful to know when you wrote it, so you could add the date to the name: *Enghwk-myholsessay-21.08.06*.

Of course, it wouldn't help much if you file it in the wrong place, so you would expect to file this essay in the *Homework* folder in the *English* folder in the *School* folder. Give it the right name and keep it in the right place and you'll be able to find it again very easily. Your computer will have a search engine to help you find documents, but you should still want to have your files stored properly.

Backing up

If you use your computer a lot, you'll have lots of important information and work saved on it. That means you have something else to worry about. What if the computer crashes and all your data is lost?

Every now and again, this does happen and it's a real headache when it does. But you can make sure you are not caught out this way. Always keep a *back-up* of your stuff. This is very easy to do and quite inexpensive. If you are not sure what is involved, ask your teacher who will explain about pen drives and other storage systems.

Getting organised

Doing your own investigating and researching on the internet

The internet is a fantastic tool for investigating and researching work. It will soon be our most important resource for finding things out. Learning how to use the internet will be an essential skill as you go through school and maybe college and university and in work.

However, you do need to be careful:

✔ There is *nasty* stuff on the internet, things that are very unpleasant that only sad people would want to read about.

✔ There is *dangerous* stuff on the internet, information which would have been better never seen because in the wrong hands it could be misused for criminal purposes.

✔ There is a tremendous amount of *rubbish* on the internet. It comes in three types:

1   real rubbish, stuff that is just silly and worthless, a complete and utter waste of time

2   rubbish that has been written by some individual or a group of people for a sinister reason. There are websites that deliberately twist information to try to persuade you to believe something. For example, certain websites try to encourage racial hatred by distorting the real facts.

3   rubbish that isn't meant to be, but is. You have to be particularly careful with this sort.

Imagine you have been asked to find out about the Planet Mars for a school project. You switch on your computer and you go on to the internet. You must now call up a search engine like Google or Yahoo, and type in Planet Mars – what do you get?

You could get a site that fits into category 1 above. It should be obvious to you. Then you might get a site from category 2, in which certain facts are twisted to try to persuade you that there are Martians who are about to invade the Earth. You must give such nonsense a wide berth.

But what if you then come across an essay on Mars that seems to be just right. Be careful! Check who wrote the essay. Was it the work of the Astronomer Royal (who knows what he's talking about!) or was it the work of a ten year old in Chicago who thought it would be fun to post his essay on the internet? This kid probably knows less than you do about Mars!

So always be careful with information you get from the internet. Always try to find out where it came from and always ask yourself, 'Is this likely to be reliable?' For any project you are doing, a good starting point is the BBC (**bbc.co.uk**). The BBC site has a vast amount of information covering a huge variety of subjects. It is very reliable and it will point you in the direction of other good sites and books.

Don't just copy!

One more point about researching on the internet. When you do find good information you must put it into your own words for your school project and you must say where it came from. Cutting and pasting an article from the internet and pretending that it is your own work is a waste of your time and your teacher's time. You will be learning nothing. You might get away with it once or twice but eventually you will be caught and you will get nothing for your project. (Do it at university, by the way, and you could get thrown out. You have been warned.)

Communicating with people who have similar interests to you

In the same way as you have to be careful about information you find on the internet, you also need to be careful about talking to people on the internet.

Compared with writing a letter, it is great to be able to communicate immediately with people who live miles away, sometimes on the other side of the world. The trouble is that you can easily find yourself in touch with a stranger who is not all he or she seems. If you are emailing a friend, then you know with whom you are dealing. But if it is someone you have never met or seen, you can't be sure they really are who they say they are.

To be safe on the internet:

✔ do not get into one-to-one email correspondence with strangers,
✔ never give out personal details on the internet
✔ never arrange to meet a person you do not know.

The *good* side of electronic communication is that you can discuss things with your friends and share interests with people who have the same hobbies as you.

Email is like sending an electronic letter. Either you or your family should get one or more email addresses. They are mostly free.

MSN and other systems allow you to chat with friends. This can be great fun, but **never** use the system to be unpleasant or to bully people. There are also internet message boards where you post messages on all sorts of topics that anyone can read and reply to. The CBBC website has a good selection of message boards.

With the help of your parents and your teachers, you have to learn how to separate the good from the bad on the internet.

Dos and don'ts about computers and the internet

✔ You must be able to use computers and the internet properly and safely.
✔ You will get most benefit if you keep your computer tidy and well organised
✔ Always back up your work
✔ Never abuse other people over the internet..

ACE Skills

If you can get yourself well organised, you will be helping yourself in a whole lot of ways. You will certainly help yourself learn more successfully, both in and out of school. You'll also find that when you've got your stuff sorted efficiently, you will have more time to get on with other things. You will be a more confident individual.

You will be well placed to help others, in your family and in your community too. You will be the one who can find the lost bit of paper, the one who can remember a key bit of information, the one who has the good idea. You will be seen as an effective contributor, at school, at clubs and when people are just socialising together. If you like having your own things neat and tidy, you will want to see your town and community looking smart as well. A responsible citizen likes to see where they live looking neat and tidy and wouldn't drop litter or vandalise other people's property.

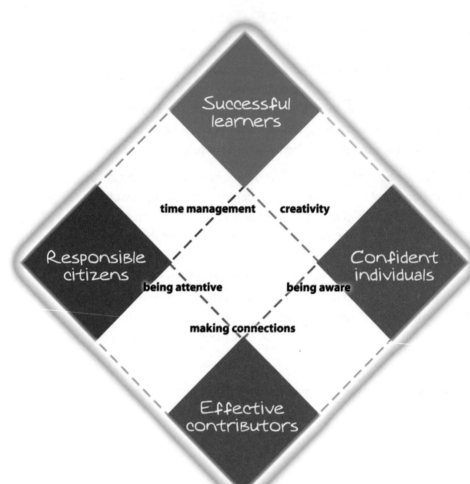

Putting it all together

You have now have learned about how your brain and body works and you have explored some ideas on how to get yourself better organised so that you can do well at school and lead a healthy life. What are you going to do now? In this chapter you will read about:

✔ time management so that you can get the most out of 24 hours in the day

✔ creativity because it is important that people have good ideas and are able to express them

✔ being attentive because we all learn so much more successfully if we are in an alert state when we are receiving new information

✔ being aware because that is part of being a responsible citizen

✔ making connections because it is when you can apply what you know in a different place or at a different time that real learning takes place.

As you think about these matters, and try to apply some of the ideas to your own life, you will continue to feel more confident about yourself. You will understand how important good learning is and become committed to being a successful learner for the rest of your life. You will also want to become a good citizen who will make responsible contributions.

Time management

Time management is about making the most of the hours in the day and the days in the week, and feeling at the end of the year that you have made good use of the previous twelve months.

At your age, you shouldn't have to worry too much about time management just yet, but you will manage your time better than most if:

✔ you use some of the advice in the last chapter to get yourself organised,

✔ you keep your diary properly, and

✔ you make these things a habit.

Work, rest and play

All of us need to work, we have to rest and we deserve some time to play. Let's look at work, rest and play and ask ourselves if we are getting the balance right

Work for you equals school and that accounts for about eight hours a day, if you include time for doing your homework. You should work hard for this time. The more you learn, the more interesting everything becomes. The more attention you pay when you are first told something, the easier it is to understand it and remember it. Don't mess about and waste time in school. There is nothing to be said for being ignorant. Study hard and you will enjoy school a lot more.

Homework

What about homework? Good homework definitely has a purpose and it ties in with the work that has been done in class. It reinforces what you have been learning and gives you the opportunity to show that you have understood what you have been taught. It is important, therefore, and the way to deal with it is to get on with it. Keep putting it off and you are just wasting your own time and perhaps storing up problems for later on.

Sleeping is good for you!

Sleep is when your brain and body gets a chance to rest. You need about eight hours sleep every night, so that your body can recover from everything you do during the day. Going to bed at a sensible time is not old-fashioned or fussy - it is paying attention to what is best for you. Are you getting your eight hours? If you are not, you are doing yourself no favours at all.

It's eight hours of sleep you need, not eighteen!

And playing is good for you!

Doing your own thing after school and at weekends is really important. Even after all your school work, and eating and sleeping and getting to and from school, there's still plenty of hours left to get on and have a good time doing the things you want to do.

There's nothing wrong with choosing to watch television and play computer games, unless you spend too much time sitting in front of a screen. You're not helping develop your brain as much as it could if you just let your entertainment be provided for you all the time. That's what happens with the television – all you have to do is sit there and watch the screen. You don't have to do much thinking for yourself.

Getting involved in sports and activities with other people is good for your brain and your body. You have to take decisions and you often have to cooperate with others, and your body enjoys being active. Hobbies like biking, skating, model-building, bird-watching or the Cadets make more demands on you, but they are probably better for you and are likely to give you more real enjoyment than any 'couch potato' entertainment.

Get the balance right

However you choose to spend your time, do try to get a good balance in your life. Get your sleep, but also take plenty of exercise. Work hard at school, but take time off as well. Have some time to yourself and with friends, and get into some activities you can get really enthusiastic about.

Having a good mixture of things to do is best when you are young. When you are older you will know better whether you want to concentrate on one thing in particular, perhaps so you can become really good at it.

Pay attention!

The biggest waste of everyone's time – parents, teachers, pupils – is lack of attention. What happens when people do not pay attention, in the classroom and elsewhere?

✔ Things are only **half understood** and a lot of extra work is needed to get a proper understanding.

✔ Completely the **wrong idea is learned** and then it takes a very long time to *unlearn* it, in order to move forward again.

✔ **Misunderstandings arise**, sometimes leading to quarrels and unhappiness, because the whole story has not been listened to and someone has jumped to the wrong conclusion.

✔ **Exams are failed**, not because you don't know the answer, but because you have misread the question and not answered what you were asked.

✔ **Accidents happen** and people get hurt because warning signs have been ignored or someone has allowed their attention to slip.

✔ **Games are lost** because, for example, in a football match the goalkeeper who has played well for 89 minutes suddenly stops paying attention and throws away a goal in the last minute.

We could all think of lots more examples of when lack of attentiveness can lead to problems.

Attentiveness is about concentration. It is astonishing how much you can learn, and how quickly you can learn it, when you really concentrate. These tips will help you learn how to concentrate.

✔ Tell yourself that what you are going to do or learn is **very interesting**.

✔ **Empty your mind,** for the moment, of everything else. Close your eyes, take three or four deep breaths and relax.

✔ **Think about what you are being told or shown.** How does it tie in with what you already know, how might this information or skill be used in the future, what is your opinion on the ideas being presented to you?

✔ **Make an effort to remember what you are learning.** Could you make a list of the key facts? Could it be turned into a mindmap? When could you practise what you are learning?

✔ **Ask questions.** If there is something you are not following, do not be shy or embarrassed. Ask your teacher, parent or coach to go over the point again so that it is clearer to you.

Being attentive actually **buys you time.** You will find homework easier and quicker to do. Revision for exams will be much less painful, and you won't find yourself getting into quarrels with other people or receiving punishment exercises and detentions from your teachers. Being very attentive at the time when you are expected to learn something will make you much **more successful** and **confident** and it will mean you have more time to do the other things in your life, like thinking about the weekend, the next football match, your boy or girlfriend and what is on television tonight.

Creativity

Creativity is about **having ideas.** You cannot be too young to have ideas and you can never have enough ideas. The best way to have a good idea is to have lots of ideas. Most of them will probably go nowhere, but a few will turn out be very exciting and very precious.

This is important because so much depends on new ideas. Think about it. We need them for:

✔ **Music** Imagine if you had to listen to the same old songs. It would be very boring if we did not have new tunes and new bands to listen to.

✔ **Books** It's good to go back to old favourites but we also want new stories. What a shame if J K Rowling hadn't had the idea to write about Harry Potter.

✔ **Film and television** Don't you get bored quite quickly with repeats? They're okay sometimes, but it's good to see new shows and new characters and new stories.

✔ **Making a living** We all rely on businesses having things to buy and sell to keep the country going. Now that places like China, India and other countries in Asia make a lot of things more cheaply than we can here, it's very important to keep thinking of new things that only we can make and other countries will want to buy.

✔ **Solving the world's problems** How are we going to cure cancer and put an end to the AIDS epidemic? How can we rescue the millions of people who live in terrible poverty around the world? What are we going to do when the world runs out of oil? Is it possible to save our planet from climate change and global warming? These are gigantic challenges facing us all and to tackle them we need new ideas. You never know which is going to be the one that does the trick - perhaps the person sitting next to you in class is going to be the person who finds a cure for cancer. Perhaps it will be you! Creativity – having new ideas – is really important for all of us.

Don't be afraid of having your own ideas. We need everyone to be creative. We want lots of new ideas. Make sure you make your contribution.

www.leckieandleckie.co.uk

All of us have a lot more ideas than we realise.
There are also ways you can boost your creativity. Have a look at the
Creativity download in the ACE Study Skills pages on the Leckie and
Leckie Learning Lab website and try some of the ideas suggested to help your
creativity. Share some of your ideas with classmates and see which ones work
best. Different people will have different ways of thinking of new things
– just because your friend thinks of different things doesn't mean your ideas
are better or worse than theirs. They're just different. Some of the
most creative people are just a bit different!.

Being aware

Being aware means looking round about you and taking notice of other
people, of the place you live in, of the country you belong to and of the planet
you share with six billion other human beings. When you are young you think
mostly about yourself. As you grow up you are expected to be more aware, to
look around you a bit more, and to become what we call a responsible citizen.

Putting it all together

A responsible citizen does:

✔ try to help others
✔ take part in community activities
✔ take a pride in their home town and country.

A responsible citizen does not:

✔ drop litter
✔ do graffiti
✔ upset or threaten other people.

There is more, however. There are major threats to the Planet Earth, which you and your generation will have to cope with.

✔ There is terrible poverty in the world. Some people are very well off and you are one of these; most people are desperately poor and have a miserable life.
✔ Drugs can bring great relief to sick people but drugs are also abused and are the cause of a lot of crime and suffering.
✔ The wildlife of the planet is under threat. Many species are dying out.
✔ The climate is changing because of global warming and that is going to cause huge difficulties for many countries.
✔ Some the planet's resources are beginning to run out. For example, oil will probably run out in your lifetime.
✔ There are some very dangerous diseases affecting people's health. Diseases like AIDS and malaria have killed millions of people around the world.
✔ There are wars all over the world and not enough peace. We must hope that one of these small wars does not suddenly become World War Three.
✔ Democracy, which means everyone having a say in how they are governed, is struggling to survive in some countries where dictators deny people their basic freedoms.

A responsible citizen cares about their planet and wants to use what they have learned to make their contribution to finding solutions to all these and many other problems. You could wait until you are older to find out more about the perils facing the planet. But why wait?

Making connections

Leonardo da Vinci was one of the world's greatest thinkers. He believed that everything is connected to everything else. It's certainly an interesting and very creative game to play, comparing or trying to see a link between two ideas or two objects, which seem to be completely unconnected.

As an example let us take this book and the Forth Rail Bridge. How can they possibly be compared? Well, bridging the river can be compared to bridging the gap from being a child to being an adult, which is what this book is about. The authors of the book travelled to Edinburgh by train and went over the Forth Rail Bridge. This book is about learning information and then using it. The builders of the Forth Bridge learned from an earlier disaster, when the Tay Bridge collapsed, and used their knowledge to build a far safer bridge. This book is about having ideas and the builders of the bridge were among a huge number of engineers who over the centuries kept having better and better ideas on how to build bridges. This book explains how the brain creates a network of connections, which strengthen thinking; the bridge is strengthened by a network of connecting girders.

Comparing in this way may seem silly, but it is making us *think* about what we *know*. *Thinking* helps *understanding*.

Here is another very important point. You go to school in order to learn. But learning is pointless unless you can use your classroom learning when you are away from the classroom. Here are a few examples of ways you can do this:

✔ You can use what you learn to do in mathematics to help you in the science class. Outside school, you can use your maths to lay out a garden, to work out the best buy in the supermarket, to calculate how much paint or wallpaper will be needed to decorate a room at home and so on.

✔ You might learn about the Treaty of Union in the history class and that can help you better understand Scottish politics today. It'll help you understand how the European Union works, and why there are some people in parts of Spain who want to break away from Spain and form an independent Basque country.

✔ You can use what you learn in the Biology and Home Economics classes to get yourself fitter for sport.

✔ You can use knowledge from Geography and Chemistry to reduce pollution and make your contribution to the fight against global warming.

In all these examples learning in one area is being applied elsewhere. This is when learning becomes very useful. It is also when creative ideas emerge.

So, even when what you are studying seems boring, **make the effort to make the connections**. Even if the connection you do make is as unlikely as this book and the Forth Bridge, you will be motivating yourself to keep working, you'll be helping your concentration, you will be learning faster and you will be deepening your understanding. Get connected!

ACE Skills

Everyone has to spend time at school. This ought to be a good time, when we learn a lot. But good learning is not just about remembering facts. Much more important is:

✔ thinking for yourself
✔ using your learning
✔ connecting new information and skills to what you already know
✔ continuing to learn for the rest of your life.

Doing these things will make you a successful learner and an effective contributor because you will have ideas and be able to do things which will not only help yourself but also other people, where you live and elsewhere. If you can manage your time and be positive about your life you will feel happier and healthier and, some scientists believe, you will also live longer. Every community needs its citizens to care about each other and to behave responsibly. It is good to be a confident individual and not someone who always feels bad or unsure about themselves. But remember that being confident doesn't mean you should be cocky or cheeky or think you can do anything and get away with it.

If you can also share these ideas with others and help *them* become positive and in control of their lives, then *you* will feel even better about yourself. Everyone will win ... and that can't be bad!

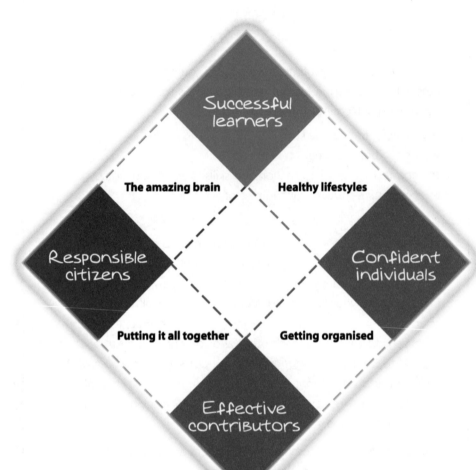

The key messages of this book are:

- ✔ Know about your **brain**
- ✔ Keep it **busy** and **stimulated**
- ✔ Know about your **body**
- ✔ Look after it with **sensible exercise** and **healthy eating**
- ✔ **Get yourself organised** at home and in school
- ✔ **Work hard** but ...
- ✔ Lead a **balanced life** with time for eating, sleeping , pursuing interests and relaxing
- ✔ **Learn about happiness** and be happier for knowing how it works
- ✔ **Be positive** and **confident** about yourself and your life.

Become:

- ✔ a Successful Learner
- ✔ a Confident Individual
- ✔ an Effective Contributor
- ✔ a Responsible Citizen.